TABLE OF CONTENTS

artwork from Book #09531

Spring & Summer

April Showers

Be my Valentine

Bunny and Me Welcome Thee

Bunny Crossing

Carrot Patch

Easter Greetings

Every Bunnies Welcome

Give hugs... if you "carrot" at all!

Happy Easter

Happy Hoppers

Happy Valentine's Day

Have a Candy Egg Easter
and a Jelly Bean Spring!

Have an Eggstra Special Day

Hop on In

Hoppin' down the Bunny Trail

Hoppy Easter

Hugs and Kisses

I believe in the Easter Bunny

I'm a good egg, just a little cracked!

Loving you Dear Valentine

Put all your eggs in one basket
and give the basket to God

Somebunny Cares

Spring has Sprung

Summer Delight

Summer's Joy

The voice of Spring

Think Spring

Together is the nicest place to be!

Tweet Yourself

....

....

....

....

....

....

....

....

....

....

....

The Fall Season

artwork from Book #09531

A crow lives here

Autumn Greetings

Autumn's Praise

Be Thankful

Best Witches

Blessed are the Turkeys

Caution - Ghost Crossing

Country Harvest

Gather a Harvest of Love

Give Thanks

Happy Fall

Happy Halloween

Happy Harvest

Happy Haunting

Happy Haunts

Happy Thanksgiving

Happy Turkey Day

Harvest Greetings

Harvest Time

Harvest Welcome

If the Broom fits.... Fly it!

Keeper of the Crows

Let's talk Turkey

No Crows Allowed

Pumpkin Patch

Pumpkins for Sale

Share the Harvest

Something to Crow about

Trick or Treaters Welcome

Welcome Fall

Welcome to our Pumpkin Patch

....

....

....

....

....

....

....

....

....

Wintertime

Cold hands... Warm heart

....

Dashing through the Snow

....

I love snowy days,
frosty nights and warm hearts

....

It's Snow Much Fun

....

It's Snow Time Folks

....

Let it Snow

....

Snow Time

....

Snow Day

....

Snow Cones 5¢

....

Snowmen will melt your heart

....

Think Snow

....

Warm toes and tummies

....

Warmest thoughts and wishes
still keep us close in heart

....

Winter Garden

....

Winter Wonderland

....

Winter's Song

....

....

....

4th of July & Patriotic

FLAG RULES

Our flag should be treated with respect

Never let it touch the ground

Never let the sun set on it

Always hang flag so that the stars
are on your left when you look at it

The color red is for courage,
white is for purity and blue for loyalty

America, you're beautiful

America....
Home of the free and the brave

Bless those who serve our country

Country

Freedom

God Bless America

God Bless the USA

Happy 4th of July

Hatched in the USA

Let Freedom Ring!

Liberty

Old Glory

Sweet Land of Liberty

This land is your land

Tweet land of liberty

....

....

....

....

....

....

....

....

....

....

....

Christmas

"A" is for angel...
Especially at Christmas

A Merrie Olde Christmas

Angels are among us

A star for luck... an angel for guidance

Be naughty and save Santa a trip!

Beary Christmas

Believe in the Magic

Berry Christmas

Bottle the Joy of Christmas
throughout the year

Christmas brings hearts together

Christmas cheer "reigns" here

Christmas comes from the heart

Christmas cookies and holiday hearts...
that's the way the holiday starts

Christmas Countdown

Christmas is a Claus for Celebration

Christmas is for Children

Christmas is for Kids

Christmas is holly with berries
of red and the heavenly fragrance
of warm gingerbread

Christmas is sharing, loving and caring

Christmas Joy from head to toe

Christmas Love with all the trimmings

Christmas Memories

Come let us adore him

Countdown to Christmas

Country Christmas

Country Christmas Blessings

Dear Santa.... I Want It All

Don't let the holidays get you down

Down Home Christmas

Dropping in for the Holidays

Even though the holidays
will find us far apart...

Families are a special part of Christmas

Fill your holiday with hugs and kisses

Friends are a special part of Christmas

Friendship is the thread that ties
all hearts together at Christmas time

Glide through the holidays

Glory to the new born king

Good Cheer

Good friends share love
and memories at Christmas

Greetings

Hang on for the Hollydays

Happy Holidays

Hark the Angels

Have a "Beary" Merry Christmas

Have a Jolly Christmas

Have you been naughty or nice?

He's making a list and checking it twice

Here Comes Santa

Home for the Holidays

Homemade Cookies

Homemade goodies warm the heart

I believe in Christmas

I believe in Santa Claus

I bring you tidings of great joy

I love Christmas!

I love snowy days,
frosty nights and warm hearts

I'll play my drum for him

I'm dreaming of a White Christmas

It won't be long until Santa comes!

Jesus is born

Jesus is the heart of Christmas

Jesus, the reason for the Season

Jolly Christmas

Joy

Joy is the spirit of Christmas

Joy to the World

Joyous Noel

Just say "Ho"

Keeping the Christmas spirit

Kiss me "Deer"

Let us keep Christmas the old
fashioned way...with love in our
hearts

Let's meet under the mistletoe

Little town of Bethlehem

Love is the music of Christmas

Love... Joy... Peace... Hope

Magical Christmas

Make a joyful noise

Make Merry

May Christmas be evergreen
in your heart

May the bounty of the season fill
your heart and your home

May the love and light of Christ
our Lord fill your heart and home

May the warmth of your heart
draw near at Christmas

May you find joy in the season,
the fellowship of friends
and the closeness of family

May your Christmas be bright

May your every wish come true

Merry Chris-moose!

Merry Christmas

Merry Christmas to all!

Merry Christmas...
from our house to yours

No humbugs allowed

Noel

North Pole Bed & Breakfast

O Holy Night

O Christmas Tree

Oh Come All Ye Faithful

Oh Tannenbaum

Peace on Earth

Plaid Tidings

Reindeer Crossing

Rejoice

Remember the reason for the season

Ring those Christmas bells!

Rockin' around the Christmas tree

Santa Claus is coming to town

Santa Collector

Santa Stops Here

Santa's Helper

Santa's on his way

Santa's Workshop

Seasons Greetings

Sharing our Christmas together

Sharing our season together

Sing a song of joy

Silent Night, Holy Night

Sleigh Parking

Star light, Star bright

Surrounded with Joy

The stockings were hung
by the chimney with care

The wonder of Christmas

There's no place like
Home for the Holidays

This house believes in Santa Claus

Tho' far and wide on Earth we roam, at
Christmas time our hearts come home
Though distance may separate... the
heart remembers at Christmas

'Tis the Season

'Twas the night before Christmas

Unto us a child is born

We believe in Christmas

We believe in Santa Claus

We have seen his star

We love Christmas

We're dreaming of a White Christmas

Welcome to my Christmas kitchen

Who needs Santa... I have Grandma

Who needs Santa... I have MasterCard!

Who needs Santa... I have Visa!

Wishing you a Christmas wrapped
in Joy and filled with Love and Laughter

Wishing you a Ho! Ho! Ho!

With Christmas Love in our Hearts

....

....

....

....

....

....

....

....

Valentine's Day

Be my love

Be my Valentine

Happy Valentine's Day

Hugs and Kisses

Loving you, Dear Valentine

You're no bunny 'til
somebunny loves you

Your somebunny special!

I saw a cupid in the sky,
his magic arrow caught my eye,
he shot at me from up above,
now my heart is filled with love

Sealed with a Kiss

Together is the nicest place to be

To thee with love

....

....

....

....

....

....

St. Patrick's Day

Best O'Luck

Feelin' Irish

Happy St. Patrick's Day!

The Luck of the Irish

Top of the morning

....

....

....

....

....

The Family

artwork from Book #09531

MOTHERS

A mother is the
best friend you can have

A mother is someone who can take
the place of all others, but whose
place no one else can take.

A mother is someone
you never outgrow your need for

I picked a very Special Mom

If mothers where flowers I'd pick you!

"M" is for mom... not maid

Mama don't allow no poutin' here

Moms add lovin' spoonfuls

Moms make Memories

Mom is Busy...Take a Number

Mom's stressed...Hugs Help!

More than merely a mother...
slightly less than a God!

Mother is another name for love

Mother's are special angels

Mothers are special... especially mine!

Mothers hold their children's hands
for awhile... their hearts forever

Mothers and daughters become closer
when daughters become mothers.

Mothers are special blessings

Sometimes angels
are disguised as mothers

There's a special place in heaven
for the mother of three boys
(change the number as you wish)

We laugh, we cry, we make time fly,
best friends are we, my mom and I

A MOTHER'S WORK IS NEVER DONE
I will not have a temper tantrum
nor stomp across the floor...

I will not pout, scream or shout
or kick against the door...

I will not throw my food around
nor pick upon another...

I'll always try to be real good
because I am the Mother

WORLD'S GREATEST MOM
Who has given all,
seeking none in return?

Who patiently taught,
while I struggled to learn?

Who means the world
and loves to the end?

This someone is you,
my mother... my friend

MOTHER'S MOTTO

Cooking and cleaning
and mending too,

Are menial tasks I have to do.

But loving my children
and making them smile

Makes everything
else all worthwhile.

....

....

....

....

....

....

....

....

....

....

....

....

....

....

....

....

....

FATHERS

A father is one
of life's special blessings

A father is someone you can lean on

A father like you is a gift from God

Dads are great

Dads are special, especially mine

Dads don't allow no poutin' here

Dads know best, but no one listens

Dad is Busy...Take a Number

Daddys are made for lovin'

Daddys are special

Daddy, some day I may
find my Prince Charming,
but you will always be my King

Daddy's little girl

Fathers are special

Happiness is having a Dad like you

Partners, Buddies, Pals

Thank heaven for Daddys

World's Greatest Dad!

....

....

....

....

....

....

....

GRANDPARENTS

Grandchildren are a gift from God

Grandfathers are Special

Grandma knows best,
but no one ever listens!

Grandmas are for loving and cookies!

Grandmas are great!

Grandmas are made for lovin!

Grandma's busy.... Take a number!

Grandma's kitchen... tasters welcome

Grandmas are special angels

Grandmothers are Special

Grandmothers are a special blessing

Grandmothers are angels in training

Grandmothers are special,
especially mine

Grandpas are great

Grandpas are made for lovin!

Grandpa's sidekick

Grandparents are God's gift to children

Happiness is having grandchildren

Put the grand into Grandparents!

Sometimes angels
are disguised as grandmothers

The best antiques are grandparents

There are many treasures
in Grandma's attic, but the
old button box is my favorite.

There's no place like home... except at
Grandma's and Grandpa's

There's no place like home...
except at Nana's and Papa's

Welcome to Grandma's house

Welcome to Grandpa's house

When things get tuff...
call 1-800-Grandma

When things get tuff...
call 1-800-Grandpa

World's Greatest Grandma

World's Greatest Grandpa

....

....

....

....

....

....

....

....

....

....

....

....

CHILDREN

A daughter is a little girl
who grows up to be your friend

A daughter is a little girl who grows
up to become a wonderful friend

A daughter is such a joy

A daughter is the
best friend you can have

A son is such a joy

Always my daughter...now my friend

Babies are life's most precious gift!

Babies are blessings from above,
they fill our hearts with lots of love

Babies are little angels from above

Childhood should be
a journey... not a race

Children are a gift from God

Dad's little angel

Daddy's little cowboy

Daddy's little cowgirl

Daughters are special, especially mine

Grandma's little angel

Grandpa's little angel

Grandpa's Sidekick

Kids are my business

Little boys are Special

Little girls are Special

Mom's little Angel

No earthly joys could bring
more pleasure than a
little boy to love and treasure

No earthly joys could bring
more pleasure than a
little girl to love and treasure

Roses 'round the door, babies
on the floor, who could ask for more?

Thank heaven for little boys

Thank heaven for little girls

To have a daughter like you is to know
a special kind of joy

....

....

....

....

....

....

....

....

....

....

....

....

....

....

SISTERS

A sister is a friend forever

Always my sister, always my friend

My sister... My best friend

Sisters are a special gift

Sisters are forever

Sisters are special friends

Sisters by heart

The road to my sister is never long
(or make sister plural)

There's no better friend than a sister!

....

....

....

....

....

....

....

....

....

....

....

....

....

BROTHERS

A brother is a friend forever

A brother is someone you can lean on

Always my brother, always my friend

My brother... My best friend

Brothers are a special gift

Brothers are forever

Brothers are special friends

Brothers by heart

I can't imagine in all the world a
better brother than you

There is no better
friend than a brother!

....

....

....

....

....

....

....

....

....

....

....

FAMILY

A cousin is a childhood playmate
who grows into a forever friend

....

A family is a circle
of friends who love you

....

A family is one
of life's special blessings

....

Families are a special blessing

....

Families are forever!

....

Families are tied together
with heart strings

....

Give me a house to call my own,
family and friends to make it a home.

....

Having someone to love is family,
having both is a blessing

....

Loving family, mine to treasure,
better than wealth of any measure

....

My family tree is full of nuts

....

Our family is a circle of strength
and love, with every birth
and every union, the circle grows.
Every joy shared adds more love.
Every crisis faced together
makes the circle stronger.

....

....

....

....

....

....

....

....

....

....

....

....

....

Love & Happiness

A friend loves at all times

A gift of love

A growing love

All things grow with love

Be my Love

Blessed are the pure in heart

Choose Thy Love... Love Thy Choice

Faith... Hope... Love

Falling in love is wonderful...
staying in love is even better

Give a gift of love

Grown in love

Having someone to love is family,
having both is a blessing

Hearts that love are always in bloom

His love will shine on you

Home is where you find
warmest love and peace of mind

House full of happiness, hearts full of love

I love you "beary" much!

I love you a whole bunch

I love you just because...

In all you dream and in all you do,
may the love you share bring joy to you.

Let love reign

Live well... Laugh often... Love much

Loads of Love

Love always endures

Love always hopes

Love always protects

Love always trusts

Love at home

Love bears all things

Love bears all things,
believes all things,
hopes all things,
endures all things,
love never fails.

Love covers all

Love does not delight in evil

Love goes on forever

Love grows between us

Love grows each time it is shared

Love grows here

Love is from above

Love is kind

Love is life's greatest treasure

Love is not easily angered

Love is not rude or self seeking

Love is patient

Love is patient, Love is kind

Love is patient, Love is kind, Love
bears all things, believes, hopes and
endures all things, Love never fails.

Love is sharing

Love is the best gift of all

Love is the glue that mends

Love is the thread of life

Love keeps no records of wrongs

Love Life!

Love lifted me

Love makes a house a home

Love never fails

Love one another

Love one another... for love is of God

Love reigns

Love rejoices in truth

Love unlocks any door

Love warms the heart

Love, Laughter and friends
are always welcome

Love does not envy or boast

Loving kindness is forever

May the hearts of this home
always be warmed by love

May you find strength
in the love that surrounds you

May you find the strength
to face tomorrow in the love
that surrounds you today.

Moments of love

My heart belongs to you

My love will never let me go

Only love can make a difference

Our friendship is tied with love

Our love is tied with heartstrings

Preserved with love

Puppy love is from above

Reflections of His love

Sending my love your way

Sharing is a gift of love

Smile, God loves you

Someday my love

Sprinkles of love

Tender loving care

The best things in life are made with love

The brightest love comes from above

Thee I love

This house... established with love

To love is nothing...
to be loved is something...
to love and be loved is everything!

We can do no great things,
only small things with great love.

Where love is, no house is too small

Wishing you a day bright with sunshine...
warm with love

You love me... I love you...
you be faithful... I'll be true

Your love is so uplifting

....

....

....

....

....

Inspirational

A friend like you is a gift from God

A friend like you is a special hug from God

A loving home is a piece
of heaven on Earth

A reflection of his love

All are precious in his sight

All creatures great and small,
the Lord God made them all

Always be full of Joy in the Lord

As for me and my house
we will serve the Lord

As for my house we will serve the Lord

Bear ye one another's burdens

Believe in miracles

Bless all

Bless our home
with happy hearts dear Lord

Bless this home

Blessed are you in the going in,
blessed are you in the going out

Cheerful giver

Children are a gift of God

Count your blessings

Don't fear tomorrow, God is already there

Every day is a gift from God,
that's why it's called the present

Every sunrise is a gift from God

Expect a miracle

Gather your dreams!

Give thanks to the Lord for
His loving kindness is forever

Give us this day our daily bread

Give your burdens to the Lord...
He will carry them

God Bless this Home

God Bless this home... A loving
home is a piece of heaven on earth

God is love

God keeps his promises

God loves you so much
he can't take his eyes off you

God understands

Hands to work...hearts to God

He careth for you

He cleansed my soul

He leadeth me

Hello Lord, it's me again

Help Lord, I'm in a spot

Hug one another

It doesn't matter where you go in life,
what you do or how much you have...
It's who you have beside you.

Jesus loves me

Jesus loves you

Kindness begins with me

Let not the sun
go down upon your wrath

Life's Precious Moments

Lord grant me patience
to endure my blessings

Lord, keep me on my toes

Lord, keep my life in balance

Love is patient, Love is kind,
Love bears all things, believes, hopes
and endures all things, Love never fails.

May the light of God's
love guide your path

May the Lord fill your life with blessings

May the warmth in your heart,
grow peace in your home

May you find strength
in the love that surrounds you

May you find the strength to face
tomorrow in the love
that surrounds you today.

Nothing can dampen the spirit of caring

Now I lay me down to sleep

Perfect harmony!

Prayer changes things

Precious moments together

Safe in the arms of Jesus

Seek and ye shall find

Sharing life's blessing

Sing to the Lord with thankful hearts

Surely... goodness and mercy
shall follow thee

The joy of the Lord is my strength

The Lord bless you and keep you

The Lord giveth, and
the Lord taketh away

The Lord will bless
his people with peace

This is your day to shine

Thou art mine

To everything there is a season
and a purpose under heaven

Today is a gift from God...thank him

Trust in the Lord with all your heart

Walking by faith

We are all precious in his sight

We are God's workmanship

With God all things are possible

Yield not to temptation

You are my happiness!

You are the end of my rainbow

....

....

....

....

....

....

....

....

From the Heart

A friend is someone
who listens from the heart

A home is a house with a heart inside

A kind word warms the heart

Bless your heart

Blessed are the peacemakers

Enter with a happy heart

Friends from the heart

Friendship starts in the heart

Friendship warms the heart

From the heart

Heart and Home

Heart to Heart

Hearts to Hearts

Hold my heart, hold my hand

Home is where the heart is!

Home is where you hang your heart

Keep in your heart a place
where dreams can grow

Keep your heart soft

Love warms the heart

May the hearts of this home
always be warmed with love

May you have warmth in your heart,
peace in your home

My heart is exposed with love

Real friends listen with their heart

Sharing comes from the heart

The best gifts are tied with
heartstrings

The heart of the home

There's a hole in my heart
when I'm far from you

Thoughtfulness always
warms the heart

You have touched so many hearts

....

....

....

....

....

....

....

....

Friendship

A friend is a gift to treasure forever

A friend is a hug to my heart

A friend is a rare book of which but
one copy is made

A friend is always within reach

A friend is one who opens
the door to home and heart

A friend is someone who cares

A friend is someone
who listens with the heart

A friend is someone who reaches
for your hand and touches your heart

A friend is someone who accepts
you just the way you are

A friend is someone you can lean on

A friend is the voice on the other end

A friend like you is a gift from God

A friend like you
is a special hug from God

A friend loves at all times

A life richly blessed is one
encircled by true friends

A real friend walks in when
the rest of the world walks out

A sister is a friend forever

A true friend is
the rarest of all blessings

Always my sister, always my friend

As treasured keepsakes warm the home,
cherished friendships warm the heart

Be kind to your friends!

Best friends always

Cherished friendships warm the heart

Choose thy friends like books...
few but choice

Dear friends gather here

Enter as strangers... leave as friends

Everything is better when
shared with a friend

Extend your hand in friendship
and give your heart to love

Fishing for friends

Forever friends

Friend to friend

Friend to friend... heart to heart

Friends and flowers make life a garden

Friends are flowers in the garden of life

Friends are for sharing hearts

Friends are forever

Friends are joined heart to heart

Friends are just a phone call away

Friends are like pockets...
everybody needs one!

Friends are like the steady flow
of a river running with you
across every rock of life,
until the current runs smoothly again

Friends are special

Friends are the best collectibles

Friends are the flowers
that bloom in life's garden

Friends are the patchwork of life

Friends are the sunshine of life

Friends bring you to the heart

Friends can always patch things up

Friends from the heart

Friends in the Lord

Friends like you are far and few

Friends never drift apart

Friends to the very end

Friends... that's us

Friendship blooms in loving hearts

Friendship hits the spot

Friendship is a treasure

Friendship is a work of heart

Friendship is made one stitch at a time

Friendship is the thread
that ties hearts together

Friendship makes everyday
a celebration of the heart

Friendship starts in the heart

Friendship warms the heart

Friendship, flowers, forever

Friendship's garden

Friendships grow
From one small seed of kindness...
friendship grows

Gather friends like flowers

Give me a house to call my own,
family and friends to make it a home

Good friends are always near

Good friends are forever

Good friends are made in heaven

Good friends are never forgotten...
they live within our hearts

Happiness is being married
to your best friend

I can't imagine in all the world
a better friend than you

I'm so glad that you are my friend

I've had many friends with whom I've
shared my time, but very few with
whom I've shared my heart.

If friends were flowers,
I'd pick a whole bunch of you!

If friends were flowers I'd pick you!

If we should live to 103,
best friends we shall still be

Life is a patchwork of friends

Little by little, day by day, friends
and flowers grow that way

Little candle in my window,
to my friends a welcome glow

Love cannot break a true friendship

Love surrounds our friendship

Love, laughter and friends
are always welcome

Make a friend today

My sister... My best friend

Neighbors by chance... friends by choice

Never close your gates to a friend

Old friends are the best friends

Our friendship is sewn in love

Our friendship is soda-licious

Our friendship is tied with love

Our friendship is very special

Rain or shine...you're a friend of mine!

Rainbow of friendships

Real friends listen with their heart

Sew nice to be your friend

Sisters are special friends

Special friends... special memories

That's what friends are for

The best antiques are old friends

The road to a friend's
house is never long

The road to a friend is never long

The seasons may come and go,
but friends last forever

There's no better friend than a sister

There's no greater treasure
than a good friend

Time and seasons change,
but not the ways of friendship

Time may pass and we may part,
but true friends stay close at heart

'Tis better by far at the
rainbow's end to find
not gold but the heart of a friend
To my forever friend

Together is the place to be

Treasured friends

True friendship is a knot
which angel hands have tied

We laugh, we cry, we make time fly...
best friends are we, my mom and I

We need a good friend
through the ruff times

Welcome Friends

When friends gather... hearts warm

You add sweetness to my life

....

....

....

....

....

....

....

....

....

....

....

Wedding & Anniversary

artwork from Book #09473

10 years and still going strong
(replace with whatever year needed)

40 Happy Years
(replace with whatever year needed)

A dream that is dreamed by two,
is a dream that will come true

Be my Love

Bless the bride, bless the bowl,
bless the biscuits, give them soul

Bless you two

Choose Thy Love - Love Thy Choice

God Bless our Years Together

God bless our years together
with so much love and happiness

Happiness is being married
to your Best Friend

Heaven bless your togetherness

In all you dream and in all you do,
may the love you share bring joy to you.

It doesn't matter where you go in life,
what you do or how much you have...
it's who you have beside you!

Marriages are made in heaven
but so are thunder & lightning

Precious Memories

Sealed with a kiss

Sharing our joy together

Sharing sweet moments together

The Lord bless you and keep you

This is the day
which the Lord hath made

To thee with love

Together is a wonderful place to be!

Together is the nicest place to be!

Two hearts as one

We're in it together

....

....

....

....

....

....

....

....

....

....

Special Folks

Anyone can drive a car, but it takes someone special to drive a bus

Hairstylists are a cut above the rest

Nurses have patients

Nurses are angels of mercy

Nursing is a work of the heart

Old postal employees never die... they just lose their zip

Secretaries are a special type

Firefighters save hearts and homes

....

....

....

....

....

....

....

....

....

....

....

....

....

....

....

....

....

....

....

....

....

....

artwork from Book #09543

Teachers

"A" is for apple

A teacher sees tomorrow in a child's eye

A wise teacher makes learning a joy

Apples and spice

Kids are my business

Little red schoolhouse

Sometimes angels
are disguised as teachers

Teach from the heart

Teacher's task - to take a lot of live wires
and make sure they're well grounded

Teachers are "beary" special!

Teachers are special

Teachers cannot live by apples alone

Teachers have Class

Teachers shape the future
one child at a time

Teachers touch Tomorrow

The hand that rocks the future

Time spent teaching is never lost

To teach is to love

To teach is to touch a life forever

To teach is to touch for eternity

World's Greatest Teacher

You are the apple of my eye

Love is
2 Touch
4 Eternity

2 Teach is
2 Touch lives
4 Ever

2 nice
2 be
4 gotten

···

···

···

···

···

···

···

···

···

···

Country Livin'

COUNTRY COMMANDMENTS

Only one God

Musn't fib or gossip

Go to Sunday meeting

Adultery forbidden

Honor Ma & Pa

Don't hanker for friend's things

No idols

Do not kill

Y'all don't cuss

Must not steal

A loving home is a piece
of heaven on Earth

Bless my country kitchen Lord,
and warm it with Thy Love

Country Angels bring Country Blessings

Country at Heart

Country Fresh

Country Harvest

Country Market

Every sunrise is a gift from God

Fresh baked

Fresh from the farm

Happy Trails to you

Home Sweet Country Home

I love Country Cookin'

I love my Country Kitchen!

I love my Country Home

To everything there is a season
and a purpose under heaven

··

··

··

··

··

··

··

··

··

··

··

Homemade

A stitch in time

Creative types are seldom tidy

Friends can always patch things up

Friends are the patchwork of life

Friendship is made
one stitch at a time

Hands to Work... hearts to God

Happiness is Homemade

Homemade

Homemade apple pie

Homemade cookies

Homemade goodies

Homemade goodies warm the heart

Homemade Lovin'

Lend a helping hand

Life is a patchwork of friends

Love is Homemade

Memories are Stitched with Love

Mother "sew" dear

Our friendship is sewn in love

Sew glad we're friends

Sew in love

Sew nice to be your friend

Those who sleep under a quilt,
sleep under a blanket of love

Threadin' our way to heaven

Thumbbody loves you!

When life gives you scraps, make a Quilt

You keep me in stitches!

....

....

....

....

....

....

....

....

....

....

....

....

Kitchen

artwork from Book #09524

A messy kitchen is a sign
of a successful meal

Apples and spice

Baked with love

Bottled with love

Canned with love

God blesses this kitchen,
but he doesn't clean it!

Grandma's busy take a cookie

Grandma's kitchen

Grandma's kitchen... tasters welcome

Happiness is lick'n the spoon

Home Cookin'

I love Grandma's cookin' best

Keeper of the Kitchen

Kitchen closed...this chick has had it!

Kitchen closed..... not in the mood

Kitchen open... now serving

Lend a helping hand

Mama's Kitchen

Nothin' says lovin' like
fresh from the oven

Scramble on in

Seasoned with sunshine

Self Service Kitchen

Sugar-n-spice makes everything nice

Tea for two

The kitchen is... the heart of the home

This chick is cookin'

This is an Equal Opportunity Kitchen

Today's Menu...
2 Choices: Take it or Leave it

Warm is wonderful

Welcome to my kitchen

You are the apple of my eye

....

....

....

....

....

....

....

....

....

....

artwork from Book #09524

In the Garden

A growing love

A sprinkle of love makes friendship grow...

All things grow in love

All things grow with love

Be gentle with our earth

Beyond the garden gate

Bloom where you're planted

Blossomland

Bouquets of happiness

Crazy about watermelon

Do gardening angels have thumbs?

Don't be afraid to go out on a limb...
that's where all the fruit is

Everything grows with a little sunshine

Everything's coming up roses

Farm fresh vegetables

Friends and flowers make life a garden

Friends are flowers in the garden of life

Friends are the flowers in life's garden

Friends are the sunshine of life

Friends are the flowers
that bloom in life's garden

Friends... flowers... forever

Friendship blooms in loving hearts

Friendship garden

Friendship grows

From one small seed of kindness...
friendship grows

Garden patch

Garden recipe...
Love and water and sunshine

Gardeners know all the dirt

Gardening...
just another day at the plant

Gardening Angel... I sprinkle seeds
over the earth that they
may bloom the promise of new life

Gather a harvest of love

Gather friends like flowers

Gather your dreams

Grow... dang it!

Grow... please!

Grown in love

Harvest seeds of love

Have a sunshine day

Hearts that love are always in bloom

Hello sunshine

Home is where you plant yourself

Home grown

How does your garden grow

I don't grow anything
in my garden but tired!

I love apples

I love sunflowers

I love you a whole bunch

I never promised you a rose garden

I'd rather be in my garden

If friends were flowers
I'd pick a whole bunch of you

If friends were flowers I'd pick you

Keep in your heart a place
where dreams can grow

Keeper of the garden

Let it shine

Little by little, day by day,
friends and flowers grow that way

Love blooms eternal

Love grows between us

Love grows each time it is shared

Love grows here

May all your weeds be wildflowers

May your day be filled with daisies

May your day be filled with roses

May your day be filled with sunflowers

May your life be filled with sunflowers

Never enough Thyme

No crow allowed

No weed please

Now the Spring angel comes
as the flowers blow in the wind
while birds gather with songs
to sing oh so sweet

Old gardeners never die...
they just go to pot!

Plant a little sunshine

Plant kindness... gather love

Plant kindness in your garden

Plant Manager

Plant seeds of kindness

Plant seeds of kindness...
gather a harvest of love

Plant the whole earth with flowers

Scatter seeds of happiness

Scatter seeds of happiness
wherever you may go

Secret garden

Seeds of kindness

Sow seeds of kindness

Sow seeds of love

Sowing the seeds of love ....

Stop and smell the roses ....

Sun shines, birds sing...
garden angels the flowers bring ....

Sunflower farms ....

Sunflower patch ....

Sweet on the vine ....

Take time to smell the flowers ....

Take time to sniff the posies ....

The earth smiles in flowers ....

The sun shines, birds sing...
garden angels take to wing ....

The sun shines, birds sing...
garden angels the flowers bring ....

Those who plant kindness gather love ....

Thyme began in a garden ....

Watermelons 5 cents ....

Watermelons are sweet ....

Watermelons are wonderful ....

Weed eater ....

Welcome birdies ....

Welcome to my garden ....

Welcome to the melon patch ....

Wherever you go, whatever you do,
may your garden angel watch over you ....

You are my sunshine ....

Welcome Signs

WELCOME
to our
HOME

artwork from Book #09524

Bless all who Enter

Bless our Cabin

Enter with happy hearts

Every Birdie Welcome

Friends are "Beary" Welcome!

Friends welcome here

God Bless our Home

Home Sweet Home

Love, Laughter and Friends
are always welcome

No matter what the season...
you're always welcome

Trick or Treaters Welcome

Udderly Welcome

Welcome Birdie!

Welcome each new day

Welcome folks

Welcome Friends!

Welcome to Grand Central Station

Welcome to my garden

Welcome to my kitchen

Welcome to our cabin

Welcome to our coop

Welcome to our home

Welcome to our neighborhood

Welcome to our patch

Welcome to the changing seasons

Welcome to the melon patch

Welcome to this dirty house

....

....

....

....

....

....

....

....

....

....

artwork from Book #09490

Animals

BEARS

Bear hugs given here

Bear hugs to you

Bear the good news

Beary Christmas!

Don't feed the bears... they're stuffed!

Everything in life I share,
except of course my teddy bear

Home is where your honey is

I have a bear from days gone by, very worn
and tattered, but it was there for me to
love and that's all that really mattered

I love bears

I love you "beary" much

There's a rip and a tear in my teddy bear...
Love pours from him everywhere!

You are "beary" special

....

....

....

....

....

BUNNIES

Feeling stressed?
Just pull out your hare!

Friends welcome "hare"

I love you a whole bunch

Oh no! A grey hare!

Some bunny's sleeping

Somebunny loves you

Somebunny Special

There's a "hare" in the tub!

Warm and wonderful

Warm is wonderful

What's wrong with one grey hare?

....

....

....

....

....

....

CATS

A house is not a home without a cat ....

Better to have a fat cat
than many mice ....

Cats are people too ....

Have a "purrfect" day ....

Here kitty, kitty, kitty! ....

Husband and Cat missing...
25 cents reward for cat ....

I Love Cats ....

If you want the best seat
in the house... move the cat ....

I'm really a tiger,
but you can call me pussycat ....

It's tough being "purr-fect" ....

Meowie Christmas ....

My cats are sunshine in my life! ....

No cats allowed ....

Paws to smell the catnip ....

The only self cleaning thing
in this house is the cat ....

The "purr-fect" friend ....

The "purr-fect" way to spend the day ....

Warm is wonderful ....

Wipe your paws ....

You never have too many cats ....

You're not somebody 'til
you're ignored by the cat ....

You read, I'll purr ....

....

DOGS

A boy's best friend is his dog ....

A house is not a home without a dog ....

A man's best friend is his dog ....

Be tuff! The "dog days"
of summer can be wuff! ....

Chasing your tail gets you nowhere...
'cept back to where you started ....

Dogs are people too ....

Dogs think they are human...
cats know they are! ....

Family and friends welcome...
Fleas are not ....

Friends Fur-ever ....

Husband and dog missing...
25 cents reward for dog ....

If you want the best seat
in the house.... move the dog ....

Life is just one
table scrap after another ....

My dog's not spoiled...
I'm just well trained! ....

No dogs allowed ....

Recycle bones here ....

When please doesn't work...Beg! ....

When the going gets tuff...
the tuff get their mummies ....

Wipe your paws ....

Wipe your paws or else! ....

....

....

COWS

"Moo"chas Gracias

A mother's love is like no udders

Back door is udderly best

Cow lovers ain't like no udder!

Cows 4-rent

From Moo to Ewe

Home is where the herd is

Just hang in with the herd

Love one an udder

Mom's udderly busy

My cow and me welcome thee

Udderly Welcome

Use Udder Door

Welcome... our guests
are like no udder

You can't have one
without the udder

....

....

....

....

....

....

....

PIGS & SHEEP

Bless Ewe!

Ewe are loved

Ewenique

High on the hog!

Hogs and kisses

Pigout or be thin

Thou shalt not swine

....

....

....

....

....

....

....

....

....

....

....

....

....

....

BIRDS

An old crow and a cute chick live here

An old crow lives here

Be like a duck... calm on the surface
and paddling like mad underneath

Beware... Attack chicken on duty!

Bless our nest

Don't ruffle my feathers (I get ugly)

Every bird loves his own nest best

Feed the birds

Hatched in the USA

Here chick... chick... chick

Home Tweet Home

How tweet it is

Kitchen closed... this chick's had it!

This chick is cookin'

Though one wears fur
and the other wears feathers;
true friends always stick together

Tweet land of liberty

Two old crows live here

Waddle I do without you?

Welcome to our coop

You're part of our flock

....

....

....

....

FUN ANIMAL SAYINGS

A busy hive, a buzzy bee,
bring sticky honey for your tea!

And they came two-by-two

Born to fish

Deer friends

Frogs are lucky,
they eat what bugs them

Recycle bones here

Were you raised in a barn?

....

....

....

....

....

....

....

....

....

....

....

....

....

Miscellaneous

artwork from Book #09524

A house becomes a home
when there's love inside

A house is built with boards and beams...
A home is built with love and dreams

A rainbow is a promise

ABC...123 this smile's
for you and it's from me

Anyone can drive a car, but it takes
someone special to drive a bus

Ark rides 5 cents

Back door guests are best

Believe the impossible

Catch a falling star

Cherish yesterday..
dream tomorrow...
live today

Clean houses never last...
hugs and kisses do

Count your blessing

Enjoy life's little pleasures

Every man's house is his castle

Everyone smiles in the same language

Everything eventually
comes out in the wash

Faith... Hope... Charity

Firefighters save hearts and homes

Fun in the sun

Give thanks for all thou hast...
live as though this day's your last

God bless the moon
and God bless me

God rest his love upon this door
and bless this house forevermore

Happiness at our fingertips

Happiness is belonging

Happiness is...

Happy days are here again

Happy trails to joy

Have a good day

Have a nice day

Have a sunshine day

Having somewhere to go is home

Hello sunshine

Hold onto your dreams

Home is best

Home Sweet Home

Hugs and Kisses

Hugs and kisses, stars for wishes

I can't spell success without you

I have a doll from days gone by,
very worn and tattered,
but she was there for me to love,
and that's all that really mattered

I like you just the way you are

I wish you all things bright and beautiful

I'll trade you smiles

If you see someone without a smile,
give him one of yours

It's what's inside that counts

Keep looking up

Keep your sunnyside up

Kindness begins with me

Let it shine

Let the whole world know

Life is to share

Little things keep life happy

Live well... Laugh often... Love much

Look for the lights of home

May your every wish come true

Moments to share

My favorite fan

Never miss a rainbow
because you're looking down

Noah and Co...Bird seed supply

Nobody's perfect

Nursing is a work of the heart

Only love can make a home

Over the rainbow

Precious treasures

Put on a happy face

Rain, rain go away
come again another day

Reach for the moon

Reach for the stars

Rise and shine

Sending you a rainbow

Sending you showers of blessings

Sharing and caring

Sharing sweet moments together

Shoot for the stars

Sit long... talk much

Smile along the way

Something's missing
when you're not around

Starlight, Starbright

Sweep all your worries away

Sweet dreams

Sweet memories

Thank you for not smoking

The flying kite up in the sky...
tells me, I can make it if I try

The hand that rocks the future

The path through life may often
roam, yet it's here that
my heart feels most at home

The woods are lovely, dark and deep ....

There's a light at the end of the tunnel ....

Thou shalt not whine ....

Thoughts of you always make me smile ....

Together is the nicest place to be ....

Train up a child in the way
he should go, and when he is old
he will not depart from it. ....

Treasured keepsakes warm the best ....

Variety is the spice of life ....

Warm is wonderful ....

What the world needs is love ....

When the situation is grave,
just lift up your spirit ....

Wish upon a star ....

Wishing you a day bright with
sunshine... warm with love ....

You add sunshine to my life ....

You add sweetness to my life ....

You are my number one ....

You put a smile in my day ....

You're as pretty as a picture ....

You're just my style ....

....

....

....

Humorous

"M" is for Mom... not maid

An apple a day keeps the doctor away

A bad day at golf is better
than a good day at work

A giggle a day keeps the glums away

All men are created equal..
All women - superior!

An old grump and a nice person lives here

Be an angel.... Don't smoke

Because I'm the mom... that's why!

Blessed are they who can
laugh at themselves, for they
shall never cease to be amused

Boring women have clean houses

Born to golf... forced to work!

Caution! Possible Flooding!

Caution! Stress Overload!

Cherish yesterday, dream tomorrow,
live like crazy today!

Don't feed the bears... they're stuffed

Everyday is wash day

Feeling stressed? Just pull out your hare!

Gardening... just another day at the plant

God grant me patience... but please hurry!

Hairstylists are a cut above the rest

Having a perfect body
isn't difficult... it's impossible!

Housework causes brain damage

Housework makes me ugly

Housework makes you ugly

Housework makes
your hare turn grey

How come there's never a weekend
around when you need one!

Husband and cat missing...
25 cents reward for cat

Husband and dog missing...
25 cents reward for dog

I am strong... I am invincible..
I am crazy... I am a working mom

I breathe, therefore I shop!

I clean my house every other day...
Today is the "other" day

I don't do mornings

I have PMS and a hand gun....
Any questions?

I love my attitude problem!

I love stress!

I usually wake up Grouchy,
but sometimes I let him sleep in

I would cook dinner...
but I can't find the can opener

I'd rather be bowling

I'd rather be fishing

I'd rather be golfing

I'd rather be hunting

If life hands you lemons... make lemonade

If you sprinkle when you tinkle,
please be neat and wipe the seat

Just say no... to housework!

Lord slow me down

Lord, if I can't be skinny,
please make my friends look fat

Love is homemade... so are the bills

Mama don't allow no poutin' here

Man cannot live on chocolate alone...
but women can!

Mirror, mirror on the wall
I'm like my mother after all!

Mom's stressed... hugs help!

My aim is to keep this bathroom clean...
your aim will help!

My memory is remarkable...
I forget everything!

Nobody's perfect

Of all the things I've lost...
I miss my mind the most

Old gardeners never die...
they just go to pot!

Old postal employees never die...
they just lose their zip!

Press button for maid service,
If no answer, do it yourself!

Secretaries are a special type

So it ain't home sweet home... adjust!

Sometimes I get
even moooore confused

T.G.I.F

The deadline for complaints
was yesterday

The hurrier I go, the behinder I get

The older I get, the better I was

The spirit is willing,
but the flesh is weak

There is no life before coffee!

This is not a democracy...
this is my kingdom

This isn't clutter,
these are my antiques

Today's menu... Eat In, Eat Out

Today's menu... Take it or Leave it

Use it up, wear it out,
make it do or do without

When in doubt, take a nap

When things get tuff
call 1 - 800 - Grandma

When things get tuff
call 1 - 800 - Grandpa

Wrinkles merely indicate
where smiles have been

Ya gotta keep goin'

....

....

....

....

....

....

45

Angels

"A" is for angel

A star for luck...
an angel for guidance

An angel in the house they say...
will guard your family night and day

An angel in the kitchen
watching the stew, blesses your
cooking and all that you do.

An angel's work is never done

An angel's work is rarely done

Angel Collector

Angel of Mercy

Angels among us

Angels are among us

Angels are everywhere

Angels are very down to earth

Angels can fly because
they take themselves lightly

Angels Gather Here

Angels on Duty

Angels sent from up above...
please protect the one we love

Be an angel... Don't smoke

Be not forgetful to entertain a
stranger for thereby some have
entertained angels unaware.

Country angels bring country blessings

Do garden angels have green thumbs?

Do not fear.. the angels are near!

Don't run faster
than your guardian angel can fly!

Evening angel with stars so bright,
keep us safe throughout the night

Goodnight sleep tight...
Angels keep me thru the night

Grandmothers are angels in disguise

Grandmothers are angels in training

Grandmothers are special angels

I am sending an angel ahead
of you to guard you along the way

I believe in angels

I believe in angels,
because I believe in God

Light fades, stars appear,
evening angels gather here

Listen for your angel

Listening hearts hear angels sing

Little angels up above...
Bless our home with lots of love!

Love is how you earn your wings

Mothers are angels in disguise

Mothers are special angels

My guardian angel

Now the spring angels come
as the flowers blow in the wind
while birds gather with songs to sing.

Nurses are angels of mercy

Our house is protected by angels

Sing choirs of angels

Snow falls, the moon peeks out,
snow angels gather 'bout

Some slip, another stumbles,
special angels never grumble

Someone to watch over you

Sometimes angels
are disguised as grandmothers

Sometimes angels
are disguised as mothers

Sometimes angels are
disguised as teachers

Special Angel, Oh so dear,
hold my loved ones ever near

Sun shines, birds sing,
garden angels flowers bring

Teachers are angels in disguise

The sun shines, birds sing,
garden angels take to wing

There is an angel watching over you,
in good times, trouble or stress,
his wings are wrapped round about,
whispering you are loved and blessed.

To angels the sky is no limit!

True friendship is a knot
which angel's hands have tied

We believe in angels

Wherever you go, whatever you do,
may the angels above watch over you

Wherever you go, whatever you do,
may your guardian angel
watch over you.

....

....

....

....

....

....

....

....

....

....

....

....

....

artwork from Book #09543

Sports

A bad day at golf is better
than a good day at work

A great fisherman lives here
with the catch of his life!

Born to fish... forced to work!

Born to golf... forced to work!

Born to hunt.. forced to work!

Fishermen gather here

Fisherman on duty

Golfers gather here

Hunters gather here

Hunter on duty

I'd rather be bowling

I'd rather be fishing

I'd rather be golfing

I'd rather be hunting

I'd rather be playing tennis

I don't mind losing
as long as I look good doing it

Love means nothing at all in tennis

Tennis players gather here

Will fish for food

Will hunt for food

Will play tennis for food

Deck the hall with lots of volleys

The biggest fish
are caught by the tale

10-s, 10-s, 10-s

....

....

....

....

....

....

....

....

....

....

....

....

....

LETTERING (more lettering on page 50)

USE PROPER SPACING...

PROPER SPACING is NOT achieved by using a ruler to measure even spaces between letters!

CORRECT SPACING is done VISUALLY.

Print out the word you are using. We have chosen the word "LAND" for our example. Notice the spacing between the L and the A. Compare that with the space between the N and the D. These differences occur just because of the letter shapes. To make lettering beautiful, your eye must determine an EQUAL SPACE between each letter. Study the examples. It is something that becomes easier the more often you do it. At first you may have to trace, erase and then trace again...just to make your word look right.

L A N D

WRONG Shows measured spacing

LAND

CORRECT Example of visual spacing

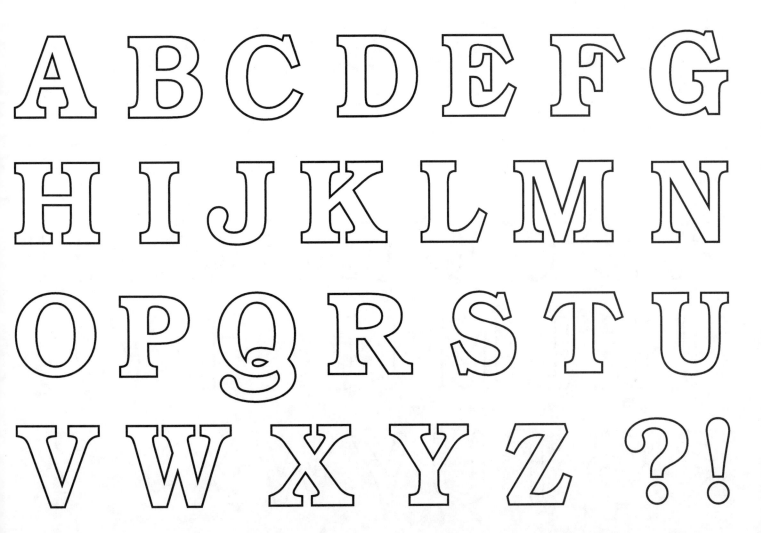

LETTERING

refer to instructions for proper spacing on page 49

a b c d e f g h i j
k l m n o p q r s
t u v w x y z ?!
1 2 3 4 5 6 7 8 9 0

A B C D E F G H I
J K L M N O P Q
R S T U V W X Y Z